Shaun White

By Matt Doeden

Lerner Publications Company • Minneapolis

Lerner Publications Company
A division of Lerner Publishing Group, Inc.
241 First Avenue North
Minneapolis, MN 55401 U.S.A.

Website address: www.lernerbooks.com

Library of Congress Cataloging-in-Publication Data

Doeden, Matt.
   Shaun White / by Matt Doeden.
      p.   cm. — (Amazing athletes)
    Includes bibliographical references and index.
    ISBN-13: 978–0–8225–6840–7 (lib. bdg. : alk. paper)
    ISBN-10: 0–8225–6840–3 (lib. bdg. : alk. paper)
    1. White, Shaun, 1986– 2. Snowboarders—United States—Biography—Juvenile literature. I. Title.
II. Series.
   GV857.S57D63 2007
   796.939092—dc22   2006009664

Manufactured in the United States of America
2 3 4 5 6 7 – DP – 12 11 10 09 08 07

TABLE OF CONTENTS

Shaun gets ready for his chance to win a gold medal.

OLYMPIC GOLD

Shaun White stood at the top of the **halfpipe**. He knew the pressure was on.

The 19-year-old was competing in the 2006 Winter **Olympic Games** in Torino, Italy. Thousands of fans were in the stands to watch this Men's Halfpipe event. Millions more were watching on TV. Shaun hadn't lost a snowboarding contest all season. But he needed a good run to make the finals. He had fallen on his first **qualifying run.** He couldn't afford any mistakes on his second.

Shaun competes in the Men's Halfpipe event at the 2006 Winter Olympics.

Shaun started his run perfectly. He was getting **big air**—making very high jumps. And he was hitting his landings. Shaun didn't do any risky tricks. He knew that a fall would end his dreams of Olympic gold. But the run was enough. The judges gave him a score of 45.3, the highest mark of the day.

Shaun soars above the crowd during his second qualifying run.

After the run, Shaun pulled off his helmet. He shook the long, curly, red hair that had earned him the nickname the Flying Tomato. "I knew that the judges wanted big and clean, and I figured that's what I'd give them," he told a reporter after the run.

The finals were up next. Each contestant would get two runs. They would each keep their best score.

Shaun landed one big trick after another. He started with a **McTwist.** Then he did a move called a **frontside 1080**. Shaun followed with a **fakie** 1080. He finished the run with a **backside** 900, then pumped his fist in the air. He knew what the screaming fans knew. It had been a great run. His score of 46.8 was the highest so far. But was it good enough to win gold?

Shaun wowed the judges in the finals.

The other riders made their second runs. But only Shaun's teammate Danny Kass's score of 43.8 came close. When Finland's Markku Koski slipped on his final run, it was over. Shaun had won the gold medal. He hugged his teammates and celebrated.

He still had to make a final run, though. Shaun just did a "victory lap," showing off for the fans. He got some big air and sprayed the stands with snow as he pumped his fists in the air. At the bottom, his eyes filled with tears as he talked to a reporter.

"It's the best year of my life," he said. "I don't think I'll ever have this again. It's amazing."

The White family *(from left)*, Cathy, Kari, Shaun, Jesse, and Roger, celebrates Shaun's gold medal.

Shaun grew up in Carlsbad, California, a suburb of San Diego.

A NATURAL

The life of the future Olympic champion got off to a rough start. Shaun Roger White was born September 3, 1986, in San Diego,

California. He was not a healthy baby. He had a heart condition called **tetralogy of Fallot.** The condition affected the oxygen supply in Shaun's blood. His parents, Cathy and Roger, had to bring Shaun in for two heart surgeries when he was very young. After the surgeries, Cathy couldn't even hold her infant son. Instead, she just held on to Shaun's tiny feet.

Shaun recovered and grew into an energetic boy. He was always on the go. He loved to surf, ski, jump on a trampoline, and play soccer. He looked up to his older brother, Jesse, and did his best to keep up.

Shaun's brother Jesse works for Burton Snowboards. He helps manage all the riders Burton sponsors. He also works with Shaun to design new snowboards and clothing.

One hobby the brothers shared was skateboarding. They spent hours learning simple tricks on the small ramp in their backyard. The family also took trips to a skiing resort at Bear Mountain in California. There, little Shaun tore down the slopes on his skis.

By the age of six, Shaun had become fascinated with the snowboarders at Bear Mountain. He wanted to learn how to ride. But

Bear Mountain is a popular skiing spot in California. Shaun admired the snowboarders there.

the resort wouldn't give lessons to anyone younger than 12. Shaun's father wanted to encourage his son. So Roger took lessons and taught Shaun how to snowboard.

Shaun's mom worried about her son. Snowboarding seemed dangerous. She told Shaun that he was only allowed to ride fakie. She hoped that making him ride backward would slow him down.

It didn't work. Shaun was a snowboarding natural. From the start, he was comfortable on the board. At the age of seven, he entered and won his first **amateur** snowboarding contest. With the win, Shaun got to compete in the 12-and-under division of the United States Amateur Snowboard Association (USASA) National Championships. Seven-year-old Shaun took 11th place. His career was off to a fast start.

Shaun's ability to get big air helped him win many trophies.

FUTURE BOY

Shaun's growing skills earned him plenty of attention. He was easily the best snowboarder in his age group. He won trophy after trophy during competitions in the mid and late 1990s. His ability to land difficult tricks and get big air helped him win five national titles in the 12-and-under division.

"I first saw (Shaun) snowboarding when he was about nine," said skateboarding legend Tony Hawk. "He was just this little pixie with a giant helmet, coming down the halfpipe. Now, he's grown into his own style—plus he can do tricks five feet higher than everyone else."

Skateboarder Tony Hawk *(below)* was impressed with Shaun's snowboarding skills.

Snowboarding wasn't Shaun's only passion. He was also becoming a skilled skateboarder. "I think that skateboarding was a way for me to kind of keep the same feeling going during the summertime," he said.

"I don't live in the mountains, and I don't constantly think about snowboarding. If I did, I would get tired of it. I'm in it all winter. By the time snowboarding is almost over, skateboarding is the light at the end of the tunnel. . . . By the time Summer X Games are over, all I can think about is getting back on the snow."
—Shaun White

Despite his great success, Shaun's snowboarding was tough on his family. As an amateur, he didn't earn any prize money for his riding. His parents spent as much as $20,000 per year on equipment, travel, and other expenses. The family often slept in their

During summers in California, Shaun would go skateboarding.

van because they couldn't afford a hotel room.

In 2000, 13-year-old Shaun decided to change that. He left the world of amateur snowboarding and turned **professional.** As a pro, he could earn money in competitions and for **endorsements**. Burton Snowboards, a popular snowboarding company, quickly signed the young star to his first endorsement deal. His family's money problems were solved.

Turning pro was a big step for such a young athlete. But Shaun quickly proved that he belonged alongside the best snowboarders in the world. He earned the nickname Future Boy. Fans and snowboarders alike could see that he was the future of the sport.

Shaun flies during the Winter X Games.

Two-Sport Star

By 2002, Shaun was no longer just the future of the sport. He had arrived. But even though he had a great year, the 15-year-old kept coming up just a little bit short. He tried to qualify for the U.S. Winter Olympic team. But he missed the cut by 0.3 points. At the Winter X Games, he finished second in both the **slopestyle** and **superpipe** events.

Tony Hawk *(left)* helped Shaun
become a professional skateboarder.

That summer, Shaun focused more on his
skateboarding. He joined Tony Hawk's Gigantic
Skatepark Tour. He rode and learned from
the best skateboarders in the world. Tony Hawk
encouraged Shaun to become a professional
skateboarder. It was an interesting idea. But
first Shaun wanted to concentrate on the 2003
snowboarding season.

It was a good decision. In 2003, Shaun dominated his competitors with huge moves and graceful 1080s. At the Winter X Games, he took gold in both the slopestyle and superpipe events. He also became the youngest rider to win the U.S. Open Slopestyle Championship. Shaun ended the season as the world's top-ranked snowboarder.

Shaun rides high to win gold medals at the 2003 Winter X Games.

Shaun enjoyed his success in snowboarding. But the idea of becoming a professional skateboarder stuck with him. He ended his 2003 snowboarding season early to get ready for his first skateboarding event as a pro. A few weeks later, Shaun finished fourth in the **vert** competition at the 2003 Slam City Jam North American Skateboarding Championships in Vancouver, Canada.

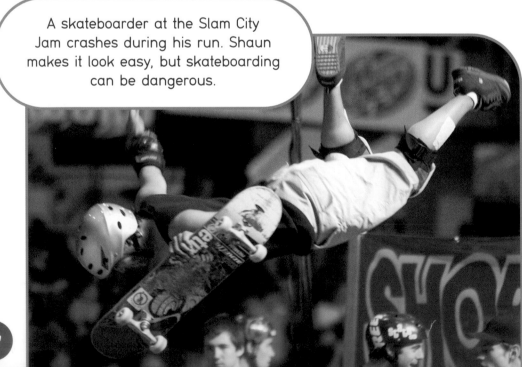

A skateboarder at the Slam City Jam crashes during his run. Shaun makes it look easy, but skateboarding can be dangerous.

The next big event for Shaun was the Summer X Games. He took sixth place in the vert competition. This was a great result for someone who spent most of his time snowboarding. For his performance in both snowboarding and skateboarding, Shaun won the ESPN "Espy" award for Best Action Sports Athlete. He had arrived as one of the biggest stars in extreme sports.

Shaun won his second gold medal in slopestyle at the 2004 Winter X Games.

STAYING ON TOP

Shaun was on top of the world. And he was still just 17 years old! What would he do next? All eyes were on him at the 2004 Winter X Games as he tried to repeat his double-gold effort of 2003.

At first, Shaun appeared to be cruising. He won the gold in slopestyle. He posted the best score in qualifying for the superpipe. But after his qualifying run, Shaun felt a sharp pain in his knee. He couldn't continue.

Shaun had surgery to repair the damaged knee that spring. Then he tried to come back before it had totally healed. He ended up hurting it again and had to sit out six more months.

"It was tough," he said. "I was really upset and didn't want to work out. I just wanted to sit there feeling sorry for myself."

By the 2005 Winter X Games, the knee was in good shape. Everyone wanted to know if Shaun was back. He didn't take long to answer that question. He scored an almost perfect 93 in slopestyle. It was his third straight gold medal in the event.

The gold medal was the start of a big year for Shaun. He won his first skateboarding vert event on the Dew Action Sports Tour. Then he took silver in the same event at the Summer X Games. With the second-place finish, Shaun became the first athlete to win a medal in both the summer and winter games.

Shaun won his first Summer X Games medal in 2005.

Shaun appeared on *The Tonight Show with Jay Leno* in February 2006.

In December, Shaun qualified for the U.S. Winter Olympic team. He was unstoppable once the 2006 snowboarding season began. He won two Winter X Games golds and had five wins on the U.S. Snowboarding Grand Prix Series. Shaun's Olympic gold was the highlight of one of the most successful snowboarding seasons in history. Fans wanted to meet him. Reporters wanted to interview him. He even appeared on *The Tonight Show with Jay Leno*.

Shaun enjoys the attention. With endorsements and other projects, he makes millions of dollars each year. He has a snowboarding DVD called *The White Album* and appeared in a **documentary** called *First Descent*. In February 2006, he signed with video

Shaun *(right)* with fellow snowboarders *(from left)* Terje Haakonsen, Nick Peralta, Hannah Teter, and Shawn Farmer at the opening of the movie *First Descent*.

game developer Ubisoft to help create a new snowboarding game.

Even with all the success, Shaun still focuses on the sports he loves. Snowboarding is an activity for the young. But during the 2010 Winter Olympics, Shaun will be just 23 years old. With a little luck and a lot of hard work, he might just earn himself another gold medal.

Selected Career Highlights

2006   Won a gold medal in the halfpipe competition at the Winter Olympics in Torino, Italy
Won his fourth straight gold in slopestyle at the Winter X Games

2005   Qualified for the U.S. Winter Olympic team
Won a silver medal in skateboarding vert to become the first athlete to earn a medal in both the Summer and Winter X Games
Won his first skateboarding gold in the vert event on the Dew Action Sports Tour
Won his third straight gold in slopestyle at the Winter X Games

2004   Released his snowboarding DVD, *The White Album*
Won gold in slopestyle at the Winter X Games before hurting his knee

2003   Took part in his first Summer X Games, placing sixth in skateboarding vert
Won his first gold medals at the Winter X Games in slopestyle and superpipe
Won the ESPN "Espy" award for Best Action Sports Athlete

2002   Took home two silver medals from the Winter X Games with second-place finishes in both slopestyle and superpipe

2001   Finished in the top ten in the slopestyle and superpipe events at the Winter X Games

2000   Accepted his first endorsement deal with Burton
Turned professional as a snowboarder

1993   Entered and won his first amateur snowboarding competition

1992   Learned to ride a snowboard

Glossary

amateur: an athlete who does not receive money to compete in events

backside: a clockwise spin (for a right-footed rider)

big air: a very high jump

documentary: a movie made about real events or people

endorsements: deals in which an athlete gets money to promote companies' products

fakie: to ride a snowboard or skateboard backward

frontside 1080: three full counterclockwise spins (for a right-footed rider)

halfpipe: a long, U-shaped ramp

McTwist: a trick in which a rider does one-and-a-half full spins while doing a front flip

Olympic Games: an event held every four years in which athletes from around the world compete in dozens of different sports

professional: an athlete who is paid to compete in events

qualifying run: the first run in a snowboard or skateboard competition

slopestyle: a snowboarding competition in which riders do tricks over a series of jumps

superpipe: a snowboarding competition in which riders do tricks on a large halfpipe

tetralogy of Fallot: a heart problem that affects the supply of oxygen in the blood

vert: a skateboarding competition held on a U-shaped vertical ramp

Further Reading & Websites

Barr, Matt, and Chris Moran. *Snowboarding*. Minneapolis: Lerner Publications Company, 2004.

Powell, Ben. *Skateboarding*. Minneapolis: Lerner Publications Company, 2004.

EXPN.com
http://expn.go.com
ESPN.com's page devoted to extreme sports has updates on many sports, including snowboarding and skateboarding.

Shaun White
http://www.shaunwhite.com/
Shaun's official site has photos and the latest news on Shaun's snowboarding and skateboarding competitions.

Index

Photo Acknowledgments

The images in this book are used with the permission of: © K.C.
Alfred/SDU-T/ZUMA Press, p. 4; © Joe Klamar/AFP/Getty Images, pp. 5, 6, 8;
© Mike Powell/Getty Images, p. 9; © Sam Wells – swellsphoto.com, p. 10; ©
Bob Rowan; Progressive Image/CORBIS, p. 12; © Kevin Zacher, p. 14; © Tom
Hauck/Getty Images, p. 15; © Tim Rue/CORBIS, pp. 17, 20; © Al Bello/Getty
Images, p. 19; © Donald Miralle/Getty Images, p. 21; © Reuters/CORBIS, p.
22; © Kevin Winter/Getty Images, p. 23; © Jed Jacobsohn/Getty Images, p.
24; © Nick Laham/Getty Images, p. 26; © NBC Universal/Getty Images, p. 27;
© Bo Bridges/Getty Images, p. 28; © Adam Pretty/Getty Images, p. 29.

Front Cover: © Rob Tringali/SportsChrome.